Faith's Heroes

Faith's Heroes

A Fresh Look at
Ten Great Christians

by Sherwood Eliot Wirt

Westchester, Illinois 60153.

CORNERSTONE BOOKS
Westchester, Illinois

The ten chapters of *Faith's Heroes* were
orginally published in *Moody Monthly* from
February 1977 through November 1978.
Copyright © Moody Bible Institute. Used by
permission.

FAITH'S HEROES:
A Fresh Look at Ten Great Christians

Copyright © 1979 by Cornerstone Books,
a division of Good News Publishers
Westchester, Illinois 60153
All rights reserved.
Printed in the United States of America.

Library of Congress Catalog Card
Number 78-71943
ISBN 0-89107-162-8

Contents

Contents

Preface

Moody Monthly readers were asking for more articles on the Great Heroes of the Faith. We knew we would have to come through, but who was qualified to write such profiles?

Anyone could research the Heroes and pull together anecdotes and quotes from musty volumes in the library. But who could make these personalities—not to mention the readers—come alive?

As I recall, it hit all of us individually on the same day. Who was the gruff but lovable dean of nearly every Christian writer's conference in the country? Wasn't it Sherwood Wirt who inspired everyone to write and who constantly quoted from St. Augustine?

And hadn't he translated Augustine's *Confessions* into modern language? Of course! The perfect choice!

Woody jumped at the opportunity. Our readers were thrilled. And you will be too as you discover and rediscover our Faith's greatest Heroes.

We're proud to say that what you'll read here originally appeared in *Moody Monthly,* and we congratulate Cornerstone Books for their foresight in putting together this beautiful book.

And it's just like Woody to somehow get himself mentioned in the same breath and always remembered with the Great Heroes of the Faith!

Jerry B. Jenkins
Executive Editor
Moody Monthly

Play The Man:

The Martyrdom of Polycarp

Chapter One

"For eighty-six years I have served my King who has saved me, and he has done me no wrong. How do you think I can blaspheme him?"

It might have been the mother of a Baptist prisoner in the Soviet Union, or an aged minister in central Africa, who spoke those words. Instead it was an early Christian, Polycarp, leader of the church at Smyrna, who was about to be made a torch for his faith.

Smyrna, known today as the Turkish seaport of Izmir, was the seat of one of the seven churches addressed in Revelation 2-3. Polycarp may well have been the "angel" of the Smyrna church mentioned in Revelation 2:8. His famous pupil Irenaeus, later bishop of Lyons in Gaul, wrote that as a young man Polycarp had known and talked with John and "the rest of those who had seen the Lord."

The story of Polycarp's unflinching witness to Christ is told in a letter written from the church of Smyrna to a sister church in Philomelium, a city of Phrygia. Known as "The Martyrdom of Polycarp," the document is universally recognized as authentic. In demonstrating the availability of grace under pressure, it is a powerful sermon. After 1800 years the testimony of the veteran follower of Jesus still comes through, telling us that God is calling Christians today to be strong, to "play the man," and to face a hostile world with faith and courage.

Polycarp suffered death in the arena in Smyrna during a persecution in 155 A.D. Here is the text of "The Martyrdom of Polycarp" as I have adapted and abridged it from the original Greek rendering and three English translations:

"Who can fail to admire the nobility of mind of the Christian martyrs of Smyrna, and their patience, and the love they showed for their Lord and Master? And especially the blessed Polycarp, who put an end to the [Roman] persecution by setting a seal upon it with his martyrdom.

"The devil invented many things against them—fire, wild beasts, beds of sharp shells—but thanks be to God, he could not prevail over any of them. Young Germanicus, for one, inspired the other Christians by his endurance, and then fought magnificently with the wild beasts. When the proconsul urged him to consider his youth, Germanicus violently dragged the beast toward himself. As a result the crowd, amazed by the heroism of the God-loving and God-fearing race of

Christians, reacted with a roar: 'Away with the atheists! [which is what the polytheistic Asians called the Christians] . Go get Polycarp! We want Polycarp!'

"When word came to Polycarp that his name was being called and that men were after him, he refused to be disturbed or flee from the city. Finally, in deference to the wish of his friends, he was persuaded to go to a farmhouse not far outside the walls. There he stayed with a few friends, spending his time in prayer for people everywhere, and for the churches throughout the world as was his custom.

"While he was praying a vision appeared to him: it seemed the pillow under his head was on fire. He turned to those with him and related the vision, adding, 'This means I must be burnt alive.'

"Three days later, as the searchers neared his hiding place, Polycarp was led secretly to another farm. Meanwhile his pursuers arrived at the first farm and seized some young slaves. Under torture, one of them revealed Polycarp's new hideout. Then, accompanied by horsemen as if they were tracking a brigand, the search party of police staked out the farm where Polycarp was lying down in an upper room. It seems he could have escaped to another place but refused, saying, 'The will of God be done.'

"When he learned that his pursuers had caught up with him, Polycarp came downstairs and talked with them. Those who were present were impressed with the man's quiet steadiness in spite of his years. Some wondered why there was so much haste for the arrest of an old man. For his part Polycarp ordered food and drink to be set before the men—all that they cared to eat—while he asked them to excuse him for an hour of undisturbed prayer. They gave him permission, and Polycarp then stood and prayed. So full was he of the grace of God that he was unable to stop for two full hours, to the astonishment of those who listened to him. Many of them repented the mission on which they had been sent.

"When Polycarp at last finished praying he was mounted on a burro and brought before Herod the Irenarch [the 'head man of peace' or chief of police in Smyrna], who took him up into the chariot in which Herod was riding with his father, Niketas. They seated him beside them and sought to win him over, asking, 'What harm is there in saying, "Caesar is Lord," in offering incense, and making sure of your own safety?'

"At first Polycarp would not answer, but as they continued to press him he replied, 'I have no intention of following your advice.' When Herod and his father saw that their efforts at persuasion were hopeless, their attitude became fierce and they shoved Polycarp out of the chariot so violently that he fell and scraped his shin. He did not turn around but walked straight toward the arena, where the uproar of the crowd was so great that no one could hear a thing.

"When Polycarp entered the stadium he heard a voice from heaven saying, 'Be strong, Polycarp, and play the man.' Some of the other Christians present heard the voice. As he was brought forward the din increased until he was presented to Statius Quadratus, the Roman proconsul. Polycarp was asked to identify himself, which he did, and the proconsul then made a fresh effort to change his mind, saying, 'You ought to have some respect for your old age.'

"The proconsul then told Polycarp to 'swear by the genius[1] of Caesar' and to 'repent and say "away with the atheists." ' Polycarp looked at the howling crowd, rolled his eyes to heaven and said, 'Away with the atheists!' The proconsul persisted, 'Revile Christ and I will let you go.' To which Polycarp made his famous reply that he had served Christ for eighty-six years and was not about to stop. Again Statius Quadratus demanded, 'Swear by the genius of Caesar.'

" 'Since you are so insistent,' answered Polycarp, 'you evidently do not know who I am. Listen plainly: I am a Christian. And if you wish to know what that is, name the day and you will hear.'

---

[1] The word relates to the Roman goddess of chance, "Fortuna."

" 'Why don't you persuade these people?' suggested the proconsul.

"Polycarp replied, 'To you I will speak, for we have been taught to honor the princes and authorities appointed by God, if our spiritual state is not hurt thereby. This crowd doesn't deserve to hear any defense from me.'

"The proconsul said, 'I have wild beasts, and I will deliver you to them unless you repent.'

" 'Bring them on,' was Polycarp's answer. 'We are not accustomed to repenting of goodness in order to do something evil.'

" 'Perhaps you would prefer the fire,' said the proconsul, 'since you despise the beasts.'

" 'Your fire burns for a while and goes out,' said the old man, 'but there is another fire you don't know about. . . . What are you waiting for? Do whatever you want!'

"Astounded, Statius Quadratus sent his herald to the center of the stadium to proclaim three times, 'Polycarp has confessed that he is a Christian!'

"The enraged crowd then shouted to Philip the Asiarch [superintendent of the sporting events] to turn loose a lion on Polycarp. Philip, however, declared that it was against the rules, since the animal sports were already ended. Then they began to cry out, demanding that Polycarp be burned alive; and their wish was carried out. Hundreds began to gather wood and faggots from the workshops and baths of Smyrna.

"When the funeral pile was ready, Polycarp took off all his clothes, including his sandals. They were about to nail him into place, but he said, 'Let me alone. He that gives me strength to endure the fire will also make it possible for me to stay in the flames without moving, and without your securing me by nails.' So they did not nail him, but simply bound him, with his hands strapped behind him; while he looked up to heaven and said, 'I give You thanks that You have counted me worthy of this day and hour. . . . I praise You, I bless you, I glorify You through Jesus Christ. . . . Amen.'

"When he had said 'Amen' and finished in prayer, the men in charge of the fire lit it and a great flame blazed up. . . .

"This, then, is the account of Polycarp, who was the twelfth to be martyred in Smyrna (counting those also of Philadelphia). . . . This took place on the second day of the month Xanthicus, the seventh day before the kalends of March, a great sabbath, at the eighth hour, when Philip of Tralles was high priest, Statius Quadratus being proconsul, but Jesus Christ being King forever, to whom be glory, honor, majesty, and an eternal throne from generation to generation. Amen."

God's Darling:

Vibia Perpetua

Chapter Two

Vibia Perpetua. The name has a familiar ring. Where have we read it—in the calendar of Roman Catholic saints, perhaps. Was she a Roman Catholic?

Vibia Perpetua would not have known the meaning of the expression. She was a Christian. She knew no other way to describe herself, though others called her God's darling.

One day Perpetua said to her pagan father, "Father, do you see this waterpot lying here?"

"I see it," he said.

"Can it be called by any other name than what it is?"

"No," he answered.

Said Perpetua, "Neither can I call myself anything else than what I am, a Christian."

All we know about this young woman is contained in an ancient document which states that Perpetua was a matron of the illustrious family of the Vibii, and that she suffered martyrdom in the amphitheater of Carthage, North Africa, on March 7, A.D. 203.

The text[1] tells us that Perpetua was "well born, liberally educated, honorably married, with an infant son at the breast, and was about twenty-two years of age." We know nothing of her husband.

The Roman authorities threw her to the beasts—in Perpetua's case a wild heifer (the Latin reads *ferocissimam vaccam*). Then they cut her throat.

So much for a brave young woman. Why speak of it now?

Because Vibia Perpetua deserves better treatment than she has received from history. She doesn't belong in a liturgical showcase, caked and crusted over by tradition. She is no relic. Her bones (wherever they are) tell us nothing. She was a beautiful, Spirit-filled person with a magnificent testimony. In this twentieth century, which has seen more martyrs for Jesus Christ than all the previous centuries together, we need to refresh ourselves with Perpetua's memory.

Septimius Severus, emperor of Rome, issued an edict in the year 202 proclaiming a persecution of Christians. Under terms of that edict Perpetua was arrested with several others, including a pregnant slave girl, Felicitas. (Perpetua's brother,

---

[1]"The Passion of SS. Perpetua and Felicitas." Three Latin texts and one Greek text are extant, all dating from around the 10th century.

also a Christian, was not arrested.)

Perpetua's own words give an authentic description of what happened next: "We were lodged in prison and I was in great fear, because I had never known such darkness. What a day of horror! Terrible heat, thanks to the crowds. Rough handling by the soldiers. And besides all this I was tormented by anxiety for my baby.

"Then Tertius and Pomponius, those blessed deacons who were looking after us, paid money to the wardens to have us removed for a few hours to a better part of the prison, where we could refresh ourselves and do what we wanted. I suckled my child who was now weak with hunger. I spoke to my mother and strengthened my brother and commended my son to their care.

"For several days after that I was upset because, for one thing, I saw that my people were upset about me. Then I obtained permission to have my baby remain in prison with me, and much of my anxiety disappeared. I recovered my health and the prison became a palace to me, so that I would rather have been there than anywhere else."

Just before she was brought before the tribunal, Perpetua's father came and knelt at her feet crying, " 'Have mercy, daughter, on my gray hair Have mercy on your father. Remember that with these hands I brought you to the full bloom of womanhood, and favored you over all your brothers. Don't shame me in front of these people. Look at your brothers, your mother, your mother's sister, your son who will die without you. Put away your pride! Don't ruin us! How could we ever speak openly among people again if anything happened to you?' "

Perpetua later wrote, "Thus did my father speak in his love for me, kissing my hands, crying and calling me not daughter, but lady. I grieved for his sake because he alone of all my relatives would not have joy in my suffering. I tried to comfort him, saying, 'Whatever happens at that tribunal will be as God chooses, for we lie not in our own power but in the power of God.' But he left me sorrowing."

On the day of the trial, Perpetua's father again begged her to offer a sacrifice for the health of the emperors which was all that the Christians were asked to do. She replied, "I won't do it." The procurator Hilarian then asked Perpetua, "Are you a Christian?" and she answered, "I am a Christian." Her father attempted to intercede but Hilarian ordered him beaten by the guard. Said Perpetua, "I grieved for my father's plight as if I had been struck myself."

Since none of the five Christians would offer the required sacrifice, the procurator condemned all to the beasts. Perpetua reported, "In hilarity we went back down to the dungeon."

Perpetua's baby boy had been placed in the

keeping of her family. She asked for him, but her father refused to give him up. As it turned out the child no longer required milk, and Perpetua discovered that she felt no anxiety in her heart, or pain in her breasts. God was preparing her for what lay ahead.

The Christians sentenced to die with Perpetua were Revocatus, a slave, Saturninus, Saturus, and Felicitas. A sixth believer, Secundulus, had been arrested, but apparently was beheaded in prison. Three days before the "games" were to begin in the amphitheater, Felicitas delivered her baby girl, a month early, in prison.

During her labor Felicitas cried out with pain, whereupon one of the wardens said, "If you are complaining now, what will you do when you are flung to the beasts?"

"Now I suffer what I suffer: but then Another will be in me who will suffer for me, because I am to suffer for him."

The English Christian writer Charles Williams has commented, "In that, Felicitas took her place forever among the great African doctors of the Universal Church."[2]

On the eve of their ordeal the five prisoners were granted the traditional public meal, all they wished to eat. These Christians turned it into a

---

[2]Charles Williams, *The Descent of the Dove*. London Pellegrini and Cudahy, 1930.

celebration and conducted an agapé (a Christian love feast).

The next morning the five went to their dungeon toward the amphitheater with light hearts, praising God. The record states that Perpetua followed last, walking meekly as one who belonged to Christ. Her appearance was so stunning that she caused many to lower their gaze.

At the gate they were told to put on special raiment: the men the robes of the priesthood of Saturn, and the women the dress of the priestesses of Ceres. Perpetua would have no part of it. She insisted that an agreement had been made that they could wear their own clothes. The tribune gave in. When she heard that he had relented, Perpetua began to sing a psalm of triumph.

Meanwhile Revocatus, Saturninus, and Saturus were brought before Hilarian the procurator. They signified to him by nods and gestures, "You are judging us, but God will judge you." This enraged the crowd and set the stage for what followed.

Roman custom called for the victims to be thrown to wild animals for a period of torture, after which they would be beheaded by a gladiator executioner. The three men were turned loose before a leopard, a bear, and a wild boar, without much of anything happening. Meanwhile Saturus (whose remarks to curiosity-seekers at the love feast the night before had won many to Christ) stopped by a gate and witnessed to the head jailer, Pudens, who later became a believer and a martyr for Christ.

Perpetua and Felicitas were stripped, forced to put on nets, and sent before a maddened cow in the arena. The audience shuddered at the sight; the women were called back and clothed in loose robes. The cow attacked Perpetua, gored her, and ripped her robe. Perpetua, more mindful of modesty than of pain, drew the robe to cover her thigh and pinned up her hair, lest anyone gain the impression that she was in mourning. Then she stood up, gave a hand to Felicitas who had also been wounded, and raised her to her feet.

Since they were not killed in the first encounter, the women were recalled to the Gate of Life—but not to live. It was a brief respite prior to execution. Perpetua spoke to her brother and to another young Christian, Rusticus, saying, "Give out the word to the brothers and sisters: stand fast in the faith, love one another, and don't let our suffering become a stumbling block to you."

Perpetua was then taken to the place of execution, the others having already been dispatched. The clumsy, untrained young gladiator thrust his sword between two bones. She shrieked. When she saw his hand wavering, Perpetua seized it and guided it to her throat.

One does not moralize about martyrs for Jesus

Christ. Perhaps a sermon Augustine preached 1,500 years ago "upon the feast of SS. Perpetua and Felicitas" best sums it up: "It is no small part of imitation to rejoice in the virtues of them that are better than we. If we may not follow them in deeds, let us follow them in affection; if not in glory, at least in gladness; if not in merits, in prayers; if not in their passion, in our compassion."

The Honest Rhetor:

Augustine

Chapter Three

He has been called the greatest African who ever lived, the keenest mind of the ancient world after Plato and Aristotle, the outstanding genius of the Roman Catholic Church, and the spearhead of the Protestant Reformation.

Austin, Texas, bears his name, as does the first city of the new world, St. Augustine, Flórida. Psychology, theology, and historical philosophy acknowledge their debt to him. For a thousand years he shaped the faith of Western Europe—until his monastic order produced Martin Luther.

Who was he?

He was Aurelius Augustinus, citizen of the Roman colony of Numidia in what is today Tunis, a teacher of rhetoric who hustled food for his Manichaean gurus, dropped his "h's," and kept a mistress.

Augustine's un-Christian activities all took place of course before his conversion; before he became the early church's prime dogmatician, controversialist and apologist; before his admirers made

29

him a priest and bishop and—God forgive them—a saint.

It was the last thing he would have wanted.

In the fall of 1941, while a student at a liberal seminary, I was assigned to write a paper on Augustine. Like any inexperienced researcher, I consulted the best secondary sources. I psychoanalyzed his conversion, documented his faults moral and otherwise, and exposed what I considered to be the weaknesses of his theological position.

How, I asked, could the man build a theology on mistranslations of Scripture? How could he box himself into a system that considered evil nothing but the absence of good, and relegated unbaptized infants to hell? How could he give tacit approval to the persecution of his enemies in the name of Christ? As far as I was concerned Augustinianism was demolished. The paper received an A+ grade.

Twenty-eight years later I consulted the primary source, Augustine himself, and for the first time I met the man. Not an interpretation of him, not a caricature of him, not a plaster saint in a cathedral niche, but a real person. Not the aging ecclesiastic who thrashed it out with the Donatists and Pelagians, but a confused, honest, and very human young person in search of God.

It was one of the great discoveries of my life. I fell in love with him. More than any Christian of his day—or for the thousand years that followed—he sounded to me contemporary. He told it the way it was.

Augustine was born in Thagaste, an inland town of North Africa, in A.D. 354. Some say he was a Berber (from the Latin *barbarian)* and some a Numidian (from which we get *nomad*). His eyes may have been blue, his skin probably was not very dark. He spoke Punic, related to the ancient Phoenician; but when he went to school, he studied Latin. He was one of three children.

Augustine's father Patricius was a poor freeman, a member of the town council, and a pagan. His mother, the celebrated Monica (actually Monnica), was a Christian. They soon recognized that they had an unusual child, and when he reached the age of ten they sent him to nearby Madaura, where for five years he received an excellent education in classical Latin. When he reached fifteen his father found it financially impossible to continue his son's education. So Augustine came home and, with nothing to do, got into trouble.

Staying out late, experimenting with sex, joining in escapades with a teenage gang, Augustine followed a career that sounds familiar to twentieth century ears. The chief motivation seems to have been his desire to be accepted by his peers. Said Augustine,

I was ashamed to be less scandalous than my

friends, whom I had heard bragging about their disgusting exploits. So I did the same things they did, not simply for the pleasure of doing them, but mostly for the praise I hoped to get. I made myself out to be worse than I was so that I might be praised for it. My invisible enemy trampled me and seduced me; and I was easy to seduce.

By the time Augustine was sixteen a wealthy friend and neighbor, Romanianus, provided a scholarship that enabled him to enroll at the University of Carthage. Here Augustine spent a dozen years, engaging in advanced studies in rhetoric, preparing for a lifework in law or government, while supporting himself by teaching. He became an accomplished scholar in what we today would call the speech and communication arts.

Carthage was then one of the flourishing cities of the Roman empire, with a population of several hundred thousand. As a center of learning, it boasted many churches, a variety of religious sects, theaters, festivals, games—and was notorious for lawlessness. Augustine sank into the worldly atmosphere of the metropolis and became a true voluptuary. He fraternized with a radical group called the "Overturners," became a neophyte of the Manichaean cult, and acquired a female companion. When he was not pursuing carnal pleasure or studying astrology, he was setting his cap to become the governor of a Roman province.

Year after year during his twenties and early thirties Augustine built his friendships and polished his eloquence. He was aiming for the top: some day, he reasoned, he would become a "friend of the emperor," the highest rank a citizen could attain.

When one reads the twenty-two books of the *City of God,* Augustine's masterpiece which took fourteen years to write, or his brilliant orthodox essay *On the Trinity,* it is hard to conceive that such works could have been produced by the pen of a passionate young African dilettante.

Ambition drove him across the Mediterranean to Italy where, after a year of teaching in Rome, he won an audition and was appointed teacher of rhetoric in Milan. He obtained the post through Manichaean connections which he continued to maintain, even though he was now disillusioned with the cult's teachings.

Christianity had played little part in his life to this point. His mother, of course, never ceased to pray for her son. She enrolled him as a catechumen in the local church during his infancy, and he was seasoned with salt according to custom. A touching passage in the *Confessions* describes his first attempt at prayer, in which he begged God to keep him from being whipped at school. Once as a boy Augustine became ill and begged to be baptized; but when he recovered quickly, his mother postponed the rite, believing it was wiser to wait until after his adolesence. She wished to take no chances with his eternal salvation.

During his years of teaching Augustine frequently encountered men of the church. Usually he held them in contempt. He talked some of his friends out of their Christian faith and read their horoscopes for them. Once in a while he would be set back, as when a friend was baptized while ill, and rebuked Augustine for making light of the sacrament; or when Augustine heard a priest speaking in public who knew how to use Scripture.

Not until he arrived in Milan, however, and began to sit under the preaching of Bishop Ambrose, did Augustine undertake to think seriously about Christianity. To that point Christ was for him a sentimental figure, venerated by his mother but ignored by the philosophers he admired. Ambrose's sermons seemed to establish in Augustine's mind for the first time a credible base for Christian belief. Some of his favorite criticisms of the Bible, which Augustine had picked up from his Manichaean friends, Ambrose showed to be straw men.

Thus began a life-and-death struggle in the soul of the young African rhetor. By reading the works of Plato's philosopher followers, notably Plotinus and Porphyry, Augustine came to realize the distinction between the spiritual and the material. By talking with some of the finest Christians of his day—Simplicianus, Vindicianus, Ponticianus, Ambrose—he received genuine encouragement. They cited examples of other men who, coming out of similar backgrounds, had chosen Christ.

Augustine was now intellectually convinced, and the issue resolved itself into a contest between two wills. A chief difficulty was that his sensual desires continued unabated. He gave up the mistress whom he had brought from Africa and who was the mother of his son, but he promptly acquired another. Before he could become a Christian, he knew he had to solve the problem of his carnality. His mother arranged a marriage, and Augustine consented; but since the girl was underage, he agreed to wait.

Such was the situation in the summer of 386. Fourteen years earlier Augustine had been strongly moved toward a life of philosophy and the contemplation of wisdom while reading Cicero's *Hortensius* (now lost). Personal ambition had stilled the impulse. Now his mistress was gone. Manichaeism and Greek philosophy no longer satisfied. His mother, having led her husband to Christ just before his death, was still praying for her son. Simplicianus had told Augustine about two members of the Emperor's secret police who had just become believers and left the imperial service.

Augustine no longer had ground to stand upon.

Going into the garden of a friend's house, he threw himself under a tree and wept. As he lay there he heard a child's voice in the adjoining yard repeating the words, "Take up and read." At first he thought it was a game, but he could recall no such game from childhood. It struck him that this was a message directed to him.

Augustine rose to his feet, walked to a table where a bound copy of Paul's letters lay open, and picked up the book. The words that he read were, "Not in rioting and drunkenness, not in chambering and wantonness, not in strife and envying, but put ye on the Lord Jesus Christ, and make no provision for the flesh, to fulfill the lusts thereof" (Romans 13:13-14).

Conversion occurred at that moment as the two wills became one. A great peace stole over the young seeker. He gave up the desires that had plagued him for years. He resigned his teaching post and, after a period of instruction, was baptized by Ambrose.

Eventually Augustine returned to Africa. His mother (who had followed him to Italy) accompanied him as far as the port of Ostia where she died, her heart's wish fulfilled. Augustine never desired to become a priest. He wanted to establish a kind of intellectual commune. But a chance visit to the coastal city of Hippo Regius resulted in his being ordained by acclamation, and within a few years the bishop of the diocese retired and Augustine was elected to succeed him.

Once appointed, Augustine set himself conscientiously to leading the flock of a fourth-rate diocese in an overseas colony. Gone was the drive of ambition; he had caught a vision of the meek and lowly Jesus, and was to spend the rest of his life contending that the original sin of man was pride.

It is said that no person has ever managed to read all of Augustine's extant writings. He took many arbitrary positions which even the Roman Catholic Church considers untenable today. His apologetic made him an uncompromising opponent. His logic forced him into a tortuous exegesis of Scripture. Many have claimed that the man was better than his theology; some have branded him an influence for evil. But the sixteenth century Reformers found his concept of "sacrament" as "sign" to be useful. It seemed to refute the doctrine of the mass, which asserted that the communion elements actually become the body and blood of the Savior.

Generally speaking, Augustine's reputation as a defender of the faith has stood the test of time, for his basic position was orthodox and sound. All of that, however, is another story. Like the rest of us, Augustine understood the mind of Christ better at some times than he did at others.

I do not consider Augustine a saint. I consider

him a friend whose personal testimony, as recorded in his *Confessions,*[1] is more honest than most (more honest than I could be); and whose devotion to his Lord has drawn me closer to the source of beauty, goodness, and truth.

[1] A fresh translation from the Latin of the autobiographical portions of the *Confessions* was published by Harper & Row in 1971 as *Love Song*. It was republished in 1977 by Zondervan as *The Confessions of Augustine in Modern English,* by Sherwood E. Wirt.

God's Troubadour:

Francis of Assisi

Chapter Four

Francis of Assisi, the Poverello, the Little Flower, the Troubadour of God. The man who kissed the leper's hand. The man who preached to the birds and wrote the Canticle to the Sun. Who doesn't love him? Who doesn't warm to his free spirit?

Undoubtedly Francis is one of the most appealing individuals to go by the name of Christian since our Lord walked the earth. How well he knew his Bible is uncertain, but what he knew, he put into practice. Born into wealth, he chose to live poor and die poor; but he made friends with God's creation and showed people how to love each other.

The Roman Catholic Church, whose loyal son he was, made a strenuous effort to accommodate him, but was never quite sure what to do with him. After Francis' death the lines were clearer; his rules were quietly laid aside, and his barefoot band of praying vagabonds became a worldwide organization of attainment and renown. The world, in its own way, has honored him by naming

41

one of its most opulent cities after him: San Francisco.

It's sad to read the closing chapters of Francis's life that tell of his disappointment with his own order and his resignation from its leadership; of his frustration at ecclesiastical encroachment; and of the bitter quarrelling that followed his death at age forty-four.

We who belong to a different tradition are all too familiar with church politics; so let us look instead at the early years. Let us watch young Francis sallying out into the world as God's knight errant, the minstrel of Jesus, frail yet strong, vulnerable yet seeming invincible in the armor of love.

Born in 1182 A.D. in Assisi, a feudal city of central Italy lying at the base of Mount Subasio, Francis was one of several sons of Pietro and Pica Bernardone. Francis was baptized Giovanni, but after Pietro, a wealthy cloth merchant, returned from one of his buying trips to France, he began calling his son Francesco (we would say "Frenchy"), and the name stuck.

Francis grew up in the narrow streets of Assisi and became known as one of the happy-go-lucky, big-spending young men of town. He was popular with the citizens for they knew him to be generous and courteous by nature. A bright future was predicted for him.

Beginning in his early twenties, a series of incidents radically changed Francis's character. First, a severe illness gave him pause to think. Later he heard God speaking to him while he was half asleep, telling him to leave the military expedition he had embarked upon and return to Assisi. Still later, in the midst of carousing, while acting as "master of the revels" for his friends, Francis fell into a mood of serious contemplation.

Some months afterward, while riding on horseback, he came upon a leper. Stifling his instinctive revulsion, Francis dismounted, kissed the leper's hand, and received in return the kiss of peace. Later he began visiting the lepers in their lazaretto.

By this time God had won his servant. Merrymaking had given way to private seasons of prayer in the forests and caves of Subasio. One day Francis was drawn to the dilapidated church of St. Damian, outside the city. Kneeling before the altar, he was told in a vision that God wanted him to repair the church.

Since the only money Francis could raise belonged to his father, a family crisis brewed. His father was outraged to learn that Francis had sold some of his cloth and given the money to the indigent priest of St. Damian. Hearing that his father was coming to fetch him, Francis fled to a cave where he hid for a month. When he appeared again in town, people who knew him looked upon him as a mental case, and the urchins tormented

him. Bernardone, learning of Francis's where-
abouts, took him home and tied him up. But when
the father had to leave the house, Pica released
her son.

Bernardone now took his case to the bishop,
who summoned Francis and asked him to give the
money back to his father. Francis did so willingly,
then stripped naked and handed his clothes also to
his father. From now on, he said, he would serve
"Our Father which art in Heaven." The bishop
covered Francis with his cloak.

Adopting a hermit's robe, Francis began walking the streets of Assisi, singing and praising the
Lord "as one drunk with the Spirit." He collected
stones and took them to the church for the recon-
struction. He begged his food and shared it with
other beggars. For a while he lived with the lepers. When the church restoration was completed,
he went to another that needed repair, and then
another.

On February 24, 1209, Francis was in the
church at Portiuncula, which he had just finished
repairing. A priest read from the tenth chapter of
Matthew: "The kingdom of heaven is at hand.
Heal the sick, raise the dead, cleanse lepers, cast
out demons. You received without paying, give
without pay. Take no gold, nor silver, nor copper
in your belts, no bag for your journey, nor two
tunics, nor sandals, nor a staff; for the laborer
deserves his food."

"This," Francis decided, "is what I want." Accordingly he discarded his staff, sandals, purse, and wallet. Making for himself a rough tunic, he used a rope for a girdle. Thus he walked about the streets and stood in the plazas of Assisi, speaking in Italian, proclaiming peace and preaching salvation through Jesus Christ. He called on the people to repent and to receive the forgiveness of sins through the cross of Christ. As always when the Gospel is faithfully declared, hearts were touched and lives were changed.

When men began to cluster around Francis, wishing to share the joy in the Spirit that he had discovered, he went to a church and opened its Bible to seek the counsel of the Lord. The passages he found were Matthew 19:21, Luke 9:1-6 and Matthew 16:24-26, all calling for renunciation and self-denial. They became the first rule of the Franciscan order.

To speak of an "order" at this time is anachronistic; these men were simply Francis's companions in the faith. They went where he went or where he told them to go. They lived in no house; they did not even stay at the Portiuncula, but walked through the countryside looking for work so they could fill the common larder. They helped peasants in the fields, then at night talked to them about Jesus. They slept in barns and haylofts, in lepers' houses, or under the porch of some church.

Barefoot, penniless, thinly clad in patched tunics and shabby drawers, singing and praying and praising the Lord, they were probably among the happiest people alive. They loved each other's company. They found much to laugh about. If they were cold, they built a fire. If there was no food, they went out and begged for it. If people tried to venerate them, they outsmarted them by such gambits as see-sawing with children. Hardship they welcomed; scandal they avoided. When they were offered money they refused it. Cares and fears were not for them; they were at peace.

But Francis, who had known the pain of opposition at home, warned his followers what they could expect; and before long the persecutions began. A dialogue between Francis and Brother Leo, one of his close friends, on the road from Perugia to Santa Maria degli Angeli, has been preserved which describes vividly the hostility they faced.

Frances talked to Leo about "perfect joy." Such joy, he said, is not found in giving "a great example of holiness and edification. " It is not in giving sight to the blind, healing the sick, giving hearing to the deaf, casting out demons, or even raising the dead. Nor does perfect joy consist (Francis continued) in speaking the language of angels, or in knowing the courses of the stars and the virtues of plants, or the qualities of birds, fishes, animals, men, trees, rocks, roots and waters. Nor does it

consist in preaching so well as to convert all in-
fidels to faith in Christ.

At this point Brother Leo said to him, "Father, I
pray you in God's name tell me in what consists
the perfect joy."

Francis replied, "When we arrive at Santa
Maria degli Angeli, soaked with rain, frozen with
cold, covered with mud, dying of hunger, and we
knock and the porter comes in a rage, saying,
'Who are you?' and we answer, 'We are two of your
brothers,' and he says, 'You lie, you are two lewd
fellows who go up and down corrupting the world
and stealing the alms of the poor. Go away.' And
he does not open to us, but leaves us outside shiv-
ering in the snow and rain till night. Then if thus
treated, we patiently endure it without murmur-
ing at him; if we think with humility and love
that this porter really knows us truly and that
God makes him speak so to us, then, O Brother
Leo, write that in this is the perfect joy."

Stories of those early days abound and make
delightful reading. When three well-known robbers came to a hermitage where a brother was in
charge, and asked for food, and were rudely
turned away, Francis (who arrived after the incident) made the brother track down the robbers,
apologize to them, pray with them and offer them
food. The robbers were not only converted, they
joined his order.

In time the Franciscan movement grew in popularity and expanded. Women formed a parallel order. Francis began sending his people to other cities, to Spain, to France, Germany, Hungary, and beyond. He even tried to carry his message of love to the Moslems, and actually preached Christ before the Sultan of Egypt, hoping thereby to bring the crusades to an end. The sultan received him courteously, heard him, and sent him back to the Christian forces.

To tell of the internal struggles of the Franciscans is not my intent. Francis's chief regret at what was happening to his order lay in the way poverty was gradually being abandoned as a thoroughgoing way of life. He was also concerned that his followers should seek no privileges from Rome. If only they would go back to the old way (he seems to be saying in his Testament) when everything went to the poor, and they worked and prayed and sang together, and were satisfied!

Nor is it my purpose to describe Francis's miraculous receiving of stigmata, or the eagerness of the people of Assisi to have him die in their city, or the relics, or the canonization that followed two years after his death.

As an evangelical Christian my heritage is the Reformation. Much as I admire the ministry of the Franciscan friars today, I do not wish to become one; nor do I aim to make Lady Poverty my bride either in principle or in fact. And yet—there is something Francis had, that Jesus had, and that I wish I had. Given the chance, as a thirteenth century Italian living in the Umbrian plain, I most certainly would have shed my sandals and gone tagging after God's Troubadour, the poor little man of Assisi, hoping to find it.

The Wild Boar:

Martin Luther

Chapter Five

What shall I write about Martin Luther, the most important European of the past thousand years? What should I write that would pass muster with ten million Lutherans around the world? What can I write, in a few words, about a man who left us ninety volumes of his own composing; who retooled the German language, reshaped its music, restructured the Christian church, and defied the mightiest powers of his day?

The life of Luther is an incredible saga. It was as if a man today were to walk into the Kremlin of Moscow alone and unprotected, and announce at the risk of his life to the assembled Congress of the Union of Soviet Socialist Republics that as a member of the Communist Party he must disobey the party's rules because the Bible is a greater authority than Vladimir Ilyich Lenin or Karl Marx.

Martin Luther is an inspiration to the free world. He is a hero to the Lutheran churches that bear his name, but he is far more. There is something of Luther in every man and woman, whether it be a Whitefield flaunting his bishop by preaching in the open fields, or a modern Catholic nun joining a march for greater freedom in the cloister. Luther himself was an Augustinian monk and a good one. He knew what it was to buck the religious establishment.

Luther cut a path through the spiritual jungle of the sixteenth century, beginning with the monastery at Erfurt, then to the pulpit at Wittenberg, and on to the confrontations at Augsburg, Leipzig, and Worms. He lived through ordeals enough to plunge anyone into pathological despair. His life was constantly threatened. Yet the effect of his achievement was to benefit Christians and non-Christians alike. Luther believed with all his heart that liberty in Christ had nothing to do with political liberation, yet he paved the way for both. He was one of the great men of all time.

Rather than retrace the oft-told story of this amazing life, I would like to assess the scope and diversity of Luther's contribution and add a few observations of my own.

First and last Luther was a man of God. The depth of his Christian experience has been matched by only a few—the Apostle Paul, Augustine, Bunyan, Pascal, Teresa of Avila, David Brainerd—none of them Germans. At some point between 1514 and 1518, while he was in his early thirties, Luther came to an awareness of the meaning of salvation through the cross of Jesus Christ. The monk who once feared the all-terrible God now discovered Him to be all-merciful. Why? Because on the cross Jesus Christ, God's Son, took to himself the iniquity of us all. He who was without sin became sin for our sakes, so that we might be forgiven, made just, blessed, and transformed from children of the devil into heirs of God.

All of this is, of course, a mystery, and it took Romans 1:17 to clear up the matter for Luther. There he discovered Paul's teaching that the just shall live by faith. And what is faith? It is, said Luther, a divine work in us which changes us and causes us to be born anew from God. Faith is a gift of the Holy Spirit through the Word of God, which frees us from sin and guilt and gives us confidence in God's grace. "Such confidence and such knowledge," Luther wrote, "makes a man joyous, gay, bold and merry toward God and all creatures." Thus Jesus Christ is the great Deliverer, not only from Satan and all his temptations, but from the bondage which holds the will in captivity to sin.

The nailing of the Ninety-five Theses of protest by Luther to the door of the Wittenberg church on October 31, 1517, is considered the opening salvo of the Protestant Reformation. However, the immediate precipitating cause of Luther's action— the scandal of indulgence-selling—was only a minor skirmish in the battle that ensued. Before long Luther was circulating violent attacks on the papacy itself and the entire hierarchical system centered in Rome. Pope Leo X responded by calling Luther a "wild boar" who had "invaded [God's] vineyard." He issued a bull of excommunication (which Luther publicly burned) and used every device to try to get this miscreant monk arrested and brought to Rome for trial.

Luther was now famous; his protest was thrusting him into the leadership of an international movement of church reform. Political circumstances created a favorable environment for his activity. His ruler Frederick the Wise, elector of Saxony, provided tolerant protection. The Holy Roman Emperor, Charles V of Spain, a fiercely loyal Roman Catholic, would gladly have crushed the "Lutheran heresy" and consigned Luther to the flames; but he was so busy fighting wars he could not spare the time. When peace was finally concluded and Charles was free to move, it was too late. Popular support had grown in Germany and the Roman Church was on the defensive.

For thirty years, until his death in 1546, Luther continued to feud with his one-time ecclesiastic superiors. He branded the pope "antichrist" and his invective found a positive response among his countrymen, particularly in northern Germany where church abuses were notorious. The Reformation spirit passed to other countries. During the years of struggle the Roman Church also sought to reform itself; but the die was cast. The church broke in two, and medievalism disappeared forever.

Some students of history believe that the church would have split whether or not Luther had lived. What makes our story interesting is that Luther (who, like the other Reformers, never intended to divide the church) did so much besides simply attack the papacy. More than any one individual he helped to fashion the character of the German people. He married a former nun and proceeded to establish a model German home, based upon love, affection, piety, and good cheer. His love for children resulted in his writing the Small Catechism, which is still in use today.

Luther's marriage at the age of forty-two was the most significant nuptial event of his time, for it marked an irrevocable break with the priestly celibacy that Rome had practiced for a thousand years. His relationship with his wife, Katharine von Bora, was a happy one; Luther called her "my lord Katie."

As a musician Luther radically reordered the church liturgy of his day. He revised the chants and chorales of the choir, and commended singing of hymns in the home after catechetical instruction. More significantly, he introduced congregational singing and himself wrote a number of hymns, including *Ein' Feste Burg* ("A Mighty Fortress Is Our God") which has been called the battle hymn of the Reformation. Luther loved music and gave it, he said, after theology, "the highest place and the greatest honor."

But even more significant was Luther's reform of the worship service itself. He essentially destroyed the mass by attacking its doctrine. The mass, he said, is not a sacrifice but a thanksgiving to God and a communion with believers. He therefore eliminated all references in the service to the priest's act of "sacrificing Christ" through the elements. With his Wittenberg colleagues Luther restored the usage of serving both bread and wine to the communicants.

By eliminating the mass Luther elevated the sermon to a place of centrality in worship. Preaching was no longer limited to a short homily, but became a vehicle of salvation through the proclaimed Word of God. Luther was a good preacher, but more important, he inspired other preachers. The typical Lutheran sermon was (and in many parts of the world still is) biblical, solemn, pious, didactic. It exhorted, sometimes castigated, but always placed a warm emphasis upon the grace of God's forgiveness and the importance of faith.

Luther was more than a musician and preacher, he was a teacher and scholar. As doctor of theology he lectured at Wittenberg University year after year. He was at home in Latin, Greek, and Hebrew; and when he was placed under house arrest for his own protection at Wartburg Castle, he undertook to translate the New Testament—and eventually the whole Bible—from the original tongues.

Luther's translation is still popular and is considered his noblest achievement. It actually shaped the German language much as the Authorized Version shaped the English language a century later. Brilliant, sonorous, earthy, devout, thoroughly Teutonic, it was a magnificent piece of work.

In addition to his translation activity Luther wrote voluminously. His tracts, pamphlets and essays found their way all over Europe. Cranmer read them in England, Calvin in France, Ochino in Italy, Valdes in Spain, Zwingli in Switzerland. His "Liberty of the Christian Man" became a classic statement of Christian truth.

Sola fide, sola gratia, sola Scriptura. (Only faith, only grace, only the Bible.) These were the watchwords of early Lutheranism. From them Luther spun out all his reforms, such as the elimination of fasting and prayers for the dead, and the reduction of the sacraments from seven to three. Two other of his teachings deserve mention, namely, the concept of Vocation or Calling, and the Priesthood of All Believers.

Luther emancipated the Christian's divine calling from the captivity of the church. Rome had taught that God called his servants to become priests, monks, and nuns; Luther declared that a milkmaid could milk cows to the glory of God. As for the priestly hierarchy, "All of us who have been baptized are priests without distinction." The husband was called to be a priest to his family as much as the pastor to his congregation. The ordination of the clergy, Luther declared, had become under Rome not a sacrament but an instrument of tyranny that turned shepherds into wolves. By recognizing the common calling of all Christians, Luther unwittingly laid the foundation for political democracy and universal suffrage.

As he often remarked, he was a miner's son and a peasant; but a day came in 1525 when he turned against the peasants, who were then in revolt. The savage words Luther spoke against them have forever damaged his name. Without condoning his passionate outburst, we can note that it would be remarkable if a man of such genius and wide-ranging influence did not show a weak side. Luther's characteristic stance was for peace and the avoidance of bloodshed. He preferred to let God have his way. Converts to faith, he insisted, could not be made by coercion; and as for heretics, they should be banished but not killed.

Reflecting upon Luther's life, I find my own spirit many times lifted up but at other times I wonder what happened to the man. Listen to these splendid words, in the very passage that warmed the heart of John Wesley 200 years later:

> Since the law is spiritual, no man keeps it, unless

everything he does comes from the bottom of his heart. But nobody has a heart like that. Only the Holy Spirit can give a man such a heart, so that he delights to keep the law.

To fulfil the law we must joyfully and lovingly do its works. But this joy, this free and voluntary love, is put into the heart by the Holy Spirit. And the Holy Spirit is not given except in, with and through faith in Jesus Christ.

The Holy Spirit makes a man's heart merry and free, as the law demands; so good works proceed out of faith. Faith is not a human notion or a dream as some take it to be; faith is a divine work in us. Oh, it is a living, creative, active, mighty thing, this faith!

No one, it seems to me, could write such words without being filled with the Holy Spirit and with love. Yet in another context Luther freely admitted that the precepts of Jesus in the Sermon on the Mount were impossible of following, even by the upright. And in still other writings Luther urged his followers to hate—*hate the pope, hate the Jew, hate the Turk, hate even the Swiss,* for he was convinced that Zwingli and the Swiss reformers (with whom he disagreed on a theological issue respecting the Communion service) were serving not God but the devil. Luther went so far as to defend his practice of cursing his enemies during his prayers, and spoke of his "unholy trinity" as consisting of the pope, the devil, and Duke George.

If you and I had been faced with the enemies that ranged against Luther on every side, we might have used even stronger language in defending ourselves. But for the past several years, I have wanted to ask Doctor Martin a question: when you told your people to hate the pope, were you aware that Jesus said we are to love men even if they are our enemies?

And if we ignore Jesus's command and don't love them then what does it mean to be a new person in Christ and filled with his Spirit? What does it mean to have faith which, Paul tells us, works by love (Galatians 5:6)? What, indeed, does it mean to be saved?

The Forgotten Reformer:

Ulrich Zwingli

Chapter Six

Baptists and Mennonites of the sixteenth century did not care for him. Pope Clement VII considered him a heretic worse than Martin Luther and excommunicated him.

Luther called him a "gross heathen" and "the devil's martyr."

John Calvin belittled him and hailed his death as a sign of God's displeasure.

The sheriff of Lucerne burned his corpse, mixed his ashes with those of a pig and scattered them in the air.

And yet in his prime this man, this Swiss, Ulrich Zwingli (Huldrych in Swiss-German vernacular), was the idol of the people and was praised and trusted as no other person of his time.

Moreover, he is probably the only one of the leading Reformers of the sixteenth century who would be welcomed warmly (and not just "honored") by today's evangelical community—including the Mennonites and Baptists.

With all his faults and weaknesses, Zwingli

remains—after William Tell—the outstanding hero of Switzerland, and is credited with laying the groundwork of the Confederation that finally united his nation in 1848.

Ulrich Zwingli was born on January 1, 1484, in a mountain village in Toggenburg valley of St. Gall canton. His father was the bailiff and he grew up in a large family. At the age of seven he was sent to school under the tutelage of an uncle, Bartholomew Zwingli. For the next fifteen years he received a remarkable education, climaxed by studies at the Universities of Vienna and Basel. He became a friend of Erasmus, the Dutch scholar and humanist. While completing his education at Basel, Zwingli came under the influence of Thomas Wyttenbach, who expounded Paul's Epistle to the Romans evangelically. Wyttenbach declared that Holy Scripture, not the pope, was the supreme authority; that only one price (Christ's) has been paid for the remission of sins—therefore indulgences were superfluous; and that remission is unlocked to the soul by the key of faith, not by the keys of Peter or of the church.

Zwingli was so inspired he agreed to become a priest, and spent the next ten years in the parish at Glarus, where he opposed the raising of mercenary troops. He finally was forced to leave, and there followed two quiet years at Einsiedeln monastery.

At Einsiedeln Zwingli was unable to rise above

the low sexual standards common among fellow clergymen. By his own admission he became involved with a barber's daughter and when in 1518 the post of people's priest became vacant in the Grossmünster at Zurich, this affair nearly cost him his candidacy. But the rival for the preaching post had a worse record (he had sired six sons) and Zwingli was elected after promising to reform.

The new preacher took the pulpit for the first time on his thirty-fifth birthday. He startled the congregation by announcing that instead of giving a homily on the liturgy of the day, he would preach his way straight through the New Testament.

Zwingli had no other blueprint or strategy, but what happened in succeeding years was consequential upon that preaching. He established himself as the authoritative voice in the city. People said of him, "He will tell us what is going on." When issues arose the city council backed the preacher.

First, Lenten fasting was abolished. Then the mercenary system was outlawed, followed by a council vote to call a halt to celibacy among priests and nuns, the worship of relics, religious street processions, the ringing of churchbells during storms, the wearing of vestments, cassocks and hoods, and the taking of fees. Images and statues were removed from churches.

Zwingli married and urged other clergy to do

the same. He shocked many by declaring that un-baptized infants that died in infancy were undoubtedly in heaven, and so were some of the pagan saints of old.

On Maundy Thursday, 1525, Zwingli did what no Roman priest had done for a thousand years. Leaving the pulpit and ignoring the high altar, he stepped down to a simple table which was covered with a linen cloth. Upon it were the vessels of communion. No silk. No silver. No golden chalice. Just wooden beakers and plates.

After facing the people and praying in his own language, Zwingli gave the elements to two deacons who, after they had partaken, went from pew to pew, serving the Lord's Supper.

Zwingli's greatest failure lay in his relations with the "Anabaptists," a small group of Christians who were convinced that the Zurich Reformation was not radical enough. They appealed to Zwingli to complete the task by abolishing infant baptism, which they declared was unscriptural. As a young priest Zwingli had leaned in their direction, but when the controversy arose in Zurich he opposed them and wrote a strong rebuttal to their views, claiming that infant baptism was simply an extension of Old Testament circumcision.

As the argument heated up, the ugly specter of religious intolerance was seen in Zurich. The cruelest joke of the Reformation was perpetrated when the council ordered Felix Manz, a young Anabaptist, to be drowned in the Limmat River. The council thought it appropriate that since Manz's "crime" was that he was rebaptized by immersion, they would execute him by drowning.

In the canton of Zurich Zwingli pioneered in social reform, had serfdom abolished, stopped street beggars, sided with the peasants in a tax struggle, and made care of the poor the concern and duty of the state. This preacher did it all without any portfolio or important position.

He overhauled the educational system of the canton and established the school of higher learning now known as the University of Zurich.

He set a pattern of worship in the Grossmünster that is still followed by non-liturgical churches in every part of the world.

He originated the Reformed system of church government characteristic of Presbyterian and Reformed Churches. (In America the Presbyterian Church constitution influenced the men who drafted the United States Constitution.)

He composed poetry, could play any musical instrument, issued a fresh edition of the poems of Pindar, and wrote the music for a performance of one of the plays of Aristophanes.

Through extensive correspondence with leaders in Italy, France, Spain, Austria, England, and Germany, he nearly brought about a Protestant political alliance that would have changed the shape of Western Europe. Instead, his political adventures were his undoing.

He created an ethic and sold it to the citizenry—but not without opposition. After his death it traveled to Geneva and then to England and New England, where it became known as the Puritan conscience.

But Zwingli was anything but a blue-nosed Puritan. His contemporaries describe him as of medium height, with ruddy countenance, level eyes, kindly face, a melodious speaking voice, and sturdy Swiss physique. They said there was nothing stilted about him; he dressed modestly and lived simply. In the pulpit he used catchy illustrations and humor—people were actually known to laugh in the cathedral! His phrases and anecdotes were frequently drawn from the native wit of Toggenburg, where he grew up.

In addition to a pleasant mien and friendly disposition, Zwingli was known for his generous spirit. He provided food for hungry children, made shelter for strangers, and gave money to help students. When Hutten, a German knight who had been banished for heresy, came to Zurich penniless and suffering from venereal disease, Zwingli at some risk found shelter for him on an island in Lake Zurich.

Today Zwingli is virtually unknown outside his own country, except by church seminary professors who frequently misinterpret his theological position.

But that would be all right with Zwingli, who was content with the fact that his name should fall into oblivion. He never reached his forty-eighth birthday. He was killed October, 1531, in a tragic battle between Swiss troops on the cantonal border of Zurich and Zug, while serving as chaplain to the Zurich contingent. It was a Catholic-Protestant struggle with political overtones, not unlike the present conflict in northern Ireland.

The Reformation did not die, and the religious lines that existed in 1531 have remained. Other leaders picked up the pieces in Zurich, Basel, Berne, and elsewhere; but the powerful voice, the radiant spirit, the free soul of Zurich was gone.

Before his death, Zwingli managed to bring about within twelve years the most astonishing change in the history of Zurich. Almost single-handedly he persuaded a medieval Roman Catholic city, one-fourth of whose land was owned by the church, to be transformed into a Puritan city. His only tool was the Bible, which he referred to as "the pure Word of God."

Monks and nuns were released from their vows, married, and became teachers. Monasteries and nunneries were converted into hospitals, orphanages, and soup kitchens. Churches were stripped of their statuary and had their interiors whitewashed. Baptism and burial fees were eliminated. Holders of church incomes were put to work. Latin prayers were abolished. And the financial operation of the diocese, with its treasury surplus, was turned over to a city council which used it for public relief. Also, prostitution was stopped, gambling forbidden, and a dress code established.

Few reminders of Ulrich Zwingli remain. A statue stands by the Limmat; a Zwingli hymn, written when he was stricken by the plague, may be found in the *Landeskirche* hymnal. His writings, his cogent expositions of Scripture, may be found on library shelves. His broken helmet is in a museum.

I like to think that it was Zwingli who gave to the English and Scottish divines the noblest line that they drafted into the Westminster Confession of Faith: "What is the chief end of man? The chief end of man is to glorify God and enjoy him forever."

A few years earlier Zwingli had written, "If God had not willed that His works should enjoy Him, He never would have called them forth from nothing. For what purpose, then, did He create them? That they might enjoy their Creator."

The Burning Heart:

John Calvin

Chapter Seven

God, the late evangelist Joe Blinco often remarked, has a disturbing habit of laying his hands on the wrong man.

It could be said that John Calvin was the wrong man. It could also be said that God laid his hands on him. A thin, timid, dyspeptic Frenchman with a scraggly beard, Calvin was basically a scholar who desired nothing better than to spend his life in libraries. Instead he was thrust against his will into the vortex of Europe's fiercest religious battles. Before he died in 1564 at the age of fifty-four he had met the challenge, overcome his opposition, and become one of the most influential figures in human history.

But at a cost. For while his brilliant teaching and writing and his devout spirit had won the respect of millions, his angry polemics, vindictive diatribes and mistakes of judgment made him one of the most maligned and vilified figures of his century.

Since apostolic times, probably no one in the

history of the Christian church has had so many enemies as Calvin. They insulted him on the streets of Geneva, set dogs at his heels and fired guns outside his house. His life was threatened. In the halls of government he was attacked not only on theological grounds, but on grounds of immorality which proved to be trumped-up charges. In any event, Calvin could respond in kind; his pen leaked a quality of vitriol that made him an opponent to be feared.

Yet there was a gentleness in Calvin not often mentioned. He knew how to retain the admiration and the affection of his friends. During the twenty-seven years he served as pastor in Strasbourg and Geneva, he showed a sensitivity and love for members of his parish that could serve as a model for today's ministers. His relations with his wife, Idelette, were tender and affectionate. In her pregnancy he was solicitous, and when their son failed to live he was heartbroken. Like his Lord, Calvin was a man acquainted with grief.

What a strange man is this—and what an impact he made on his generation. Calvin was truly the architect of the Reformation. What Luther and Zwingli created, he set in order. He provided the disorganized Protestant community with a Scriptural alternative to the overblown medieval church. He revised the worship service, introduced congregational singing, regulated church discipline, and established a representative church government. He founded the University of Geneva. He laid the forms of political liberty in the Western democracies by his insistence that God and God's Word stood above the state. Max Weber, the German social scientist, even went so far as to identify Calvin as the initiator of the "Protestant work ethic" that gave rise to capitalism.

But it was not so much what Calvin taught as the kind of people he produced that affected the future of the western world. Emile Leonard says that Calvin "invented a new kind of man in Geneva—Reformation man—and in him sketched out what was to become modern civilization." More than anyone else Calvin was responsible for the emergence of the "Puritan conscience" which budded first in Switzerland, then spread to other European countries including Britain and her colonies. "Calvinism" thus became a world force.

What was the essence of Calvinism? What was the chief characteristic of this "new man"? One might reply by quoting the five doctrinal points in the famed acronym TULIP—total depravity, unconditional election, limited atonement, irresistible grace, and perseverance of the saints. A profound admirer and disciple of Calvin in the last century, Benjamin B. Warfield of Princeton, said, "The Calvinist is the man who has seen God, and who, having seen God in his glory, is filled on the one hand with a sense of his own unworthiness

... and on the other hand with adoring wonder that nevertheless this God is a God who receives sinners."

John Richard Green describes the effect of such teaching on sixteenth-century Europe: "The meanest peasant, once called of God, felt within him a strength stronger than the might of kings. In that mighty elevation of the masses embodied in the Calvinistic doctrines of election and grace, lay the germs of the modern principles of human equality."

Election and grace, chosenness and favor. Such theological convictions were woven into the sober, hard-driving character so evident in the English Puritan, Scottish Presbyterian, French Huguenot, and Dutch Reformed immigrants arriving on the shores of the new world. They surfaced in the colonial struggles that led to the Declaration of Independence, and caused the German historian Leopold von Ranke to remark, "John Calvin was the virtual founder of America."

As for Calvin himself, this man whom Rome feared more than it did Luther was born in Noyon, Picardy, France, a loyal son of the papacy. As a boy he trained for the priesthood; later at his father's insistence he studied law at Orleans. Either during the latter period or shortly thereafter he underwent what he called a sudden and unexpected conversion experience. Not much is known about it; Calvin says simply that God "tamed him to teachableness."

Before long Calvin's views were becoming known in French Catholic circles. In 1533 his rooms were searched in Paris and his papers were seized by the Inquisition. Using an alias, Calvin went underground and began turning up in various cities in France, then in Strasbourg, Germany, and Basel, Switzerland.

During his stay in Basel the first edition of his *Institutes of the Christian Religion* made its appearance, and the world got a look at the famed doctrine of predestination which, after four centuries, is still the teaching for which Calvin is best remembered. Calvin himself was quite aware of its controversial nature; in his *Institutes* he wrote, "The human mind, when it hears this doctrine, cannot restrain its petulance, but boils and rages as if aroused by the sound of a trumpet."

While slipping members of his family out of France under a safe-conduct in 1536, Calvin found the road to Strasbourg blocked by troop movements and took a circuitous route that brought his group to Geneva, where they intended to spend the night. But when the Swiss reformer Guillaume Farel heard that Calvin was staying at a local inn he called on him and prevailed upon the young refugee to stay and help establish the Reformation in Geneva.

Farel detained him, as Calvin later wrote, "not so much by counsel and exhortation, as by a dreadful curse. . . . After learning that my heart was set upon devoting myself to private studies . . . he proceeded to utter the imprecation that God would curse my retirement if I should withdraw and refuse to help when the necessity was so urgent. . . . I was so terror-struck that I gave up the journey."

Thus the arrival of Calvin in the independent Swiss city was a fortuitous accident or an act of God, depending on the measure of one's Calvinistic inclinations. It might even be said that not only was Calvin the wrong man, but Geneva was the wrong city, since he never intended to live there and in fact never became a Genevan citizen. But a different view is held by many of us in the evangelical community. That is because Calvin's mark is still upon us. We may differ with much that he taught and did, but we cannot escape him.

During the years from 1536 until his death in 1564, Calvin exercised an increasing influence and control over the city of Geneva. During a three-year interim (1538-41) he was banished from the city and lived and taught at Strasbourg. However the syndics, or city fathers, found they could not control Geneva without Calvin's wise counsel. Embassies waited on him and begged him to return, which he did reluctantly.

Under Calvin's guidance the citizens of Geneva

turned their town of 15,000 inhabitants into a model community. Some of their laws and ordinances seem laughable today, but the fact remains that in Calvin's day no police force was necessary in Geneva. Meanwhile the word spread abroad, and other refugees began flocking to Geneva by the thousands from the persecuted lands of Europe. They sat at Calvin's feet as he taught the Bible. In all this time Calvin held no official position other than that of pastor and teacher. He avoided all signs of power and prestige, refused gifts, and lived in utter simplicity, sleeping little and eating but one meal a day because of his poor health.

The twentieth century has computerized the barbaric inhumanity of the sixteenth with the refinements of technology. Yet that does not make the earlier age less brutal; and Calvin lived in a cruel time. To retell the account of Calvin's quarrels with people who disagreed with his theological position—Sebastian Castellio, Michael Servetus and dozens of others—and of the intolerance shown not only by Calvin but by church and civic leaders all over western Europe, would be like trying to clean a cesspool.

Servetus was executed in Geneva because he questioned the Trinity. Calvin could have spared his life had he wished, but the reformer chose not to interfere. Servetus on the other hand called Calvin to his cell on the night before he was to die and asked pardon for any wrong he had done him. To this day the burning of Servetus has haunted the memory of Calvin, though most Christian leaders of that period approved the verdict.

In combing the *Institutes* I noted that Calvin spent many pages discussing the knowledge of God. Yet he made scarcely a reference to love— love for God and love for our fellow human beings—which, according to the Apostle John, is the one indispensible prerequisite to knowing God in the first place. John Calvin knew about love; he knew what Jesus taught; but he never learned to love his enemies. The gourd he left his followers had a worm in it; and in time (to borrow Oliver Wendell Holmes's picturesque figure) the deacon's wonderful one-hoss shay fell apart. So much for Calvinism in its most extreme form.

But Calvin was not an extremist, and it can be said that at its best, his work has survived magnificently. He is still honored around the world. Much of what he taught about the Bible, about culture, about human affairs has withstood the test of time. He built better than he knew.

Paul Wernle, the Swiss historian, has written of Calvin, "We are all glad, no doubt, that we did not live under his rod; but who knows what we would all be, had not this divine ardor possessed him?. . . It was he who fought on the battlefields of the Huguenots and the Dutch, and in the hosts of the Puritans."

Just before his death in 1564 Calvin summoned the ministers of Geneva to his bedside and told them, "I have always studied simplicity. I have written nothing through hatred against anyone, but have always set before me faithfully what I have thought to be for the glory of God." On the day after his death the magistrates, pastors, professors and citizens of Geneva gathered to pay Calvin homage. At his request he was buried in an unmarked grave.

In sacred art today is an emblem known as "Calvin's Crest," in which an open hand holds a burning heart.

The Flaming Sword:

George Fox

Chapter Eight

He was a large young man, powerfully built, with a long nose, small mouth, piercing eyes, and a voice like a bullhorn. He wore his hair shoulder-length and dressed in leather coat and breeches. Under the impressions of the Spirit of God he was given to eccentricities, such as striding through an English town in stocking feet, crying, "Woe unto the bloody city of Lichfield!"

People thought he was crazy, but he wasn't. He was George Fox, the first Quaker, an authentic European hero. Fox's spiritual descendants today, who call themselves "Friends," number a quarter of a million around the globe. They are known for their mild and pacific natures and their aversion to war, but in the mid-seventeenth century they weren't all that quiet. Fox's seal was a flaming sword. He considered that God had summoned him to fight "the Lamb's War" against ungodliness in the world and the church.

For their pains the early Quakers suffered as few human beings have had to suffer—and usually at the hands of church people. Those who sailed to America to make their witness were cartwhipped and tortured until the native Indians expressed shock at the white settlers' intolerance. But the Quakers stayed. When the parents were exiled or put to death, the children kept the faith. Today the social contribution of the Quakers to American life is recognized as gigantic. It is hard to conceive how our democracy could have emerged without them.

George Fox was born in 1624 in Leicestershire, England. Before he died in 1691 he was to spend six years of his life in various English prisons because of his boldness in preaching Jesus Christ and the Spirit-filled life. But at the time of his death he could count 50,000 Quakers in England and Ireland, and a number of groups in Holland, Germany and America.

But it was not Fox's movement. Rather it was a spontaneous expression of spiritual hunger in the north of England, blossoming in an environment that was not dissimilar to the American evangelical community of the late 1970's. The Puritan conscience was in force. The Bible was preached and studied. The churches were orthodox. Yet discerning spirits like George Fox sensed that a vast gulf existed between much professing Christianity and the actual manner of life. Many churchgoers had no direct contact with God and looked for none. They had been taught that what

God wished to communicate to man was contained in Scripture. Christ's work was finished on the cross.

What remained a mystery to clergy and lay people alike was the present power and ministry of the Holy Spirit. Many believers felt there must be more to the Christian life than what they saw and knew, but they didn't know where to search for it.

Enter a loud, articulate, rustic young man from Fenny Drayton who declared to everyone within earshot that he knew God not just by the Scriptures but also by direct revelation. He was no heretic; he knew his Bible well and believed it—and he had seen a vision. Years later he recorded it in his *Journal:*

> One day when I had been walking solitarily abroad . . . I was taken up in the love of God, so that I could not but admire the greatness of his love. While I was in that condition it was opened unto me by the eternal light and power, and I saw clearly therein that all was done, and to be done, in and by Christ. . . . I saw also the mountains burning up, and the rubbish; and the rough and crooked ways and places made smooth and plain that the Lord might come into His tabernacle. . . . I saw the harvest white, and the seed of God lying thick in the ground . . . and none to gather it; for this I mourned with tears. . . . The Lord's power brake forth; and I had great openings and prophecies.

To this twenty-three-year-old man the trappings and accretions of the church had come to mean nothing; personal experience of the Holy Spirit was everything. He began to call ministers "priests" and churches "steeple houses." And because many in the north counties were weary of formal emptiness and ready for spiritual reality, wherever he traveled—and he was constantly on the move—there sprang up groups of "Friends" or "Quakers," so-called because they "quaked" under the power of God.

But the Quaker movement was more than a spiritual renewal. These men and women, drawn from all walks of life, threw down a challenge to the whole British establishment—the church, the clergy, the judges, the magistrates, the landlords, the wealthy, the jailers, even Parliament. Their fearlessness in the face of suffering and punishment stands in stark contrast to our age of compromise.

They demanded reform in education, in care for the insane, in the wages of servants, in the relief of paupers, and in the treatment of slaves (though the Quaker stand on Negro slavery was not as vigorous as it would become a century later). They insisted on equality for women in a day when no one conceded it. And in all the uproar that ensued, George Fox was at the heart of the action.

Fox went to prison repeatedly because of his outspokenness inside and outside of churches.

And such prisons! Often the cells were dark, with no bench or mattress; excrement in some cases had remained for years, so that the dungeons were alive with lice and vermin. But George would not be silenced. Let him describe his visit to a church in 1648, when he was twenty-five years old:

As I was passing through the fields I was moved to go to Leicester, and when I came there I heard of a great meeting for a dispute, wherein Presbyterians, Independents, Baptists, and Common-prayer-men [Anglicans] were said to be all concerned. The meeting was in a steeple-house; and thither I was moved by the Lord God to go, and be amongst them. I heard their discourse and reasonings, some being in pews and the priest in the pulpit; abundance of people being gathered together.

At last one woman asked a question out of [First] Peter, what that birth was, viz., a being "born again of incorruptible seed, by the Word of God, that liveth and abideth forever." And the priest [minister] said to her, "I permit not a woman to speak in the church," though he had before given liberty for any to speak.

Whereupon I was wrapped up, as in a rapture, in the Lord's power; and I stepped up in a place and asked the priest, "Dost thou call this place a church? Or dost thou call this mixed multitude [of believer and unbelievers] a church?"

For the woman asking a question, he ought to have answered it, having given liberty for any to speak. But, instead of answering me, he asked me what a church was. I told him the Church was the pillar and ground of Truth, made up of living stones, living members, a spiritual household, which Christ was the head of: but He was not the head of a mixed multitude, or of an old house made up of lime, stones and wood.

This set them all on fire. The priest came down out of his pulpit and others out of their pews, and the dispute there was marred. But I went to a great inn, and there disputed the thing with the priests and professors [i.e., professing Christians] of all sorts; and they were all on a fire. But I maintained the true Church, and the true head thereof, over the heads of them all, till they all gave out and fled away. . . . Howbeit there were several convinced that day; and the woman that asked the question was convinced, and her family; and the Lord's power and glory shined over all.

In Nottingham a year later Fox was imprisoned (for the first time) for interrupting a minister's sermon. It was the beginning of an incredible series of reactions. At Thickhill, for example, when Fox stood up and spoke during the service, he reported that the clerk hit him in the face with his Bible, causing blood to flow; after which Fox was dragged out of the church, stoned, beaten, thrown over a hedge into a garden, beaten, and thrown back again.

But as he detailed the incident, "My spirit was revived again by the power of God" and "I declared unto them the word of life." When a judicial inquiry was ordered into the assault with a Bible, Fox forgave his attacker and refused to appear against him.

In addition to his behavior in churches, a controversial element in Fox's teaching caused much offense among the clergy. It involved his doctrine of the Holy Spirit, called by Quakers today the "inner light." It was not simply his claim to see something of God in every human being. It was his emphasis upon firsthand experience of the Spirit and power of God. The immediacy of God's Presence revealed inwardly to the soul, the principle of God's Truth carrying its own personal assurance, was a strange note to sound in the seventeenth century in Europe.

Yet there were those who welcomed it. As the Quaker movement gained ground, and men and women carried the message to Scotland, Wales, Ireland, and to London, new converts were made. In some cases ministers, judges, sheriffs, and even jailers who listened to the Word were won to the Quaker cause. Usually they ended by suffering persecution themselves.

George Fox, in particular, carried an air of authority that magnetized people. After he had polarized an audience, violence often ensued, and no wonder. But the real wonder is that Fox never seemed to harbor bitterness toward those who mistreated him.

At one time Fox was offered a captaincy in Cromwell's army, but declined. He made more than one contact with the Lord Protector, Cromwell, in attempts to secure the release of hundreds of Quakers in English prisons, but without success. After the restoration of the monarchy, persecution continued, but suffering only caused the movement to grow.

The story of Fox's later travels, of his strange marriage to Margaret Fell (ten years his senior), and of his care of the yearly meetings, cannot be related here. But it should be noted that George Fox was the innovator of several Quaker customs such as wearing the hat; refusing to swear an oath in an English court; the use of "plain speech" (thee and thou); conducting the silent meeting, and refusing to bear arms.

One of Fox's important acts in later years was to visit America. He spent the years 1671-72 journeying up and down the Atlantic seaboard, encouraging the little Quaker settlements that dotted the colonies, and making friendly contacts with a number of Indian tribes. When he returned to England he was again flung into prison, this time being falsely accused of breaking a law which forbade unauthorized gatherings of more than four persons.

Margaret Fox went to King Charles II to seek her husband's release, and succeeded in securing a royal pardon. This George refused to accept, saying he was guilty of nothing. The case dragged on in the courts until 1675 when he was at last released.

He lived to see the Stuarts overthrown in the Revolution of 1688 and the Quakers set free from prison. A lifetime of insults, slander, threats, blows, wounds, fever, hunger, cold, sickness, and imprisonment drew to its close early in 1691. On January 11 of that year, Fox preached a long and powerful sermon at the Gracechurch street meeting in London. Two days later he fell asleep and never awakened. He was sixty-seven years old.

But it is not so much the venerable Christian, the father of the faithful, who has left his stamp on church history, and is honored today as an instrument of social change. Rather it is the young country lad, filled with the Spirit of God, who is remembered—the one who stirred the Christian people of Nottinghamshire and Leicestershire as they have never been stirred since:

> Now was I come up in spirit through the Flaming Sword into the Paradise of God. All things were new, and all the creation gave another smell unto me than before, beyond what words can utter. I knew nothing but pureness and innocency and righteousness, being renewed up into the image of God by Christ Jesus. . . . Great things did the Lord lead me into, and wonderful depths were opened unto me. . . .

The Awakener:

George Whitefield

Chapter Nine

The scene was the spacious drawing room of the Countess of Huntingdon's home in Chelsea, London. George Whitefield was preaching to a large gathering of British aristocrats, including the philosopher-skeptic, David Hume. There came a dramatic pause; the mellow voice was silent. The evangelist then announced to the startled congregation that the angel Gabriel was about to "leave this sanctuary" and ascend to Heaven.

"And shall he ascend and not bear with him the news of one sinner amongst all this multitude reclaimed from the error of his ways?" Whitefield demanded of those present. He stamped his foot and raised his hands and eyes upward.

"Stop, Gabriel, stop!" he shouted. "Before you enter the sacred portals, carry with you the news of one sinner converted to God!"

Two centuries later people are still talking about him, this dramatic preacher who was once a bartender and busboy at the Bell Inn in Gloucester. Many are saying that he became the greatest gospeler of them all, save only the Apostle Paul himself. It is worth speculating whether as a single individual, George Whitefield (pronounced Whitfield) may have helped more people spiritually, and possibly affected more lives for good, than any Englishman or American of his generation.

From the time when, as a twenty-one-year-old ordinand, he first stepped into the pulpit of St. Mary de Crypt, Gloucester, on June 27, 1736, until the September day in 1770 when he preached his life away in Exeter, New Hampshire, he seems to have lived for one all-consuming purpose: to preach Jesus Christ and to bring men and women into a saving relationship with him. "God forbid," he once said, "that I should travel with anybody a quarter of an hour without speaking of Christ to them. Believe me, I am willing to go to prison and to death for you, but I am not willing to go to heaven without you."

During those thirty-five whirlwind years Whitefield left his impress on the destinies of Britain and America. When the Spirit of God sent the Great Awakening to the American colonies in 1740, Whitefield was used above any other human being. When the New England patriots were mustering their resources in 1770 for the struggle for independence, Whitefield prepared them spiritually for their role. Historians have called him the first real friend of the American Negro. He estab-

lished the first charity in America—an orphanage
in Georgia. He was in at the beginnings of half a
dozen American colleges, including the Universities of Pennsylvania, Princeton, and Dartmouth.
By introducing Britain to open-air evangelism
and lay preaching, he set the stage for the Wesleyan revival. He compiled a songbook to provide
music for the renewed Christians. He spent two
years at sea, crossing the Atlantic thirteen times
in flimsy ships in the interest of the gospel. He
toured America from New Hampshire to Georgia
time and again, as well as Ireland, Wales, Scotland, and even Bermuda, preaching all the way,
twenty sermons a week.

Yet despite his popularity and enormous following, plus the loving support of hundreds of clergymen on both sides of the Atlantic, George
Whitefield was calumniated as perhaps no other
figure of his era. His enemies threatened to mur-
der him and hired "hit men" to do the job. They
blew horns to drown out his message. They excommunicated him and ordered him out of town,
but he refused to go. They locked him out of their
churches and forced him to preach in the streets,
then drove him into a house and broke into the
house. They sent an army recruiter drumming
through the crowds that had come to hear him.
They hired merry-andrews to dress like the devil
and mimic him. They pelted him with dirt, eggs,
tomatoes, and pieces of dead cat. More than once

they hurled rocks at him until his head was covered with blood.

The great ones of the day—Dr. Samuel Johnson, Sir Joshua Reynolds, Alexander Pope, Henry Fielding, Oliver Goldsmith, William Hogarth, Horace Walpole, the Duchess of Buckingham—also heaped their scorn on him. But there were others who came and listened—Lord Chesterfield, Bolingbroke, Cowper, and even the Shakespearean actor, David Garrick.

In the midst of the uproar he created, Whitefield continued his peripatetic way, preaching the love of Christ, refusing to press charges against his adversaries, winning converts. He drew thousands to the fields ouside London; he invaded the collieries of Wales and the braes of Scotland. While appealing for funds for his orphanage, he emptied Benjamin Franklin's pockets. (Franklin, who tells this story, made it up by printing Whitefield's sermons.) Plantation slaves, who loved his preaching, came to him in Georgia asking, "Do I have a soul?" American Indians were objects of his loving concern; when Samson Occum, the great Indian evangelist, came to London to raise funds for his people, Whitefield took him into his pulpit.

This man, who at one time was probably the best-known person in America, was born in Gloucester as the youngest son of an innkeeper, and the scion of a distinguished family of clergymen. His father died when he was two years old, and his mother's remarriage was not a success. George grew up full of mischief. He drank, he swore and he stole; but he knew how to wait on people. When his mother learned of an opportunity for him to attend Oxford University as a "servitor," he took it eagerly. By this time his mind had turned to serious things; he began to study his Greek New Testament, to read devotional books, and to fast.

On November 7, 1732, Whitefield matriculated at Pembroke College, Oxford. In exchange for free tuition he became a lackey to older students. Longing for Christian fellowship, he learned about the famous "Holy Club" and its leaders, John and Charles Wesley, but as a servitor he was not allowed to speak to them. They, however, could speak to him; and it was not long before they invited him to their gatherings. Thus began a lifelong friendship which, though interrupted by theological quarrels, was renewed and continued until Whitefield's death.

In its early years the "Holy Club" was long on pious discipline and short on Christian experience. But in the spring of 1735, three years before John Wesley's "heart-warming" at Aldersgate Chapel, George Whitefield went through a seven-week crisis and emerged a new creature in Christ Jesus. After days and nights of tears and agony, he was filled with the Holy Spirit, born again, and set on fire for the Lord. The zeal and joy of those early days never left him.

Later that year Whitefield took his degree and after being ordained as deacon in the Church of England began preaching in various pulpits. He became a youthful phenomenon; crowds swarmed to hear him. At the Wesleys' urging, he sailed to Georgia and spent a year there, being warmly received in the colony. On his return to Britain he was ordained a priest. When he went back to America to found his orphanage at Bethesda, the Great Awakening burst into full bloom.

To describe in a few words the incredible ministry of Whitefield for the next three decades, preaching to crowds of up to 50,000 persons, filling a schedule on horseback that would kill most people in a private plane, is beyond my ability. There was a charm to his delivery, a grace, a harmony. In the wake of his messages, many a church sprang up, and many another found new life in the Spirit. But it remained for the Wesleys and their colleagues to water the seed Whitefield scattered, and to build a Christian community for the future.

Whitefield is remembered kindly today, although not many know about him. Why, then, was he so harshly attacked in his own time? It was not all the devil's work; George made some serious mistakes. For one thing, he outdid himself in giving advice—admonishing, reproving, even scolding. In one letter he lectures his mother; in another he preaches to the young lady he was thinking of marrying.

Unsolicited exhortations easily pass over into criticism. And since every critical remark he wrote was eagerly devoured by the reading public, Whitefield was time and again forced to make tearful apologies for his rash judgments and aspersions on the spirituality of other Christians.

The Christian clergy, especially, resented Whitefield's attacks, which is why so many churches were closed to his preaching. His reproof of John Wesley, who was eleven years his senior, was not in the wisest taste, even though Whitefield was on solid ground. Wesley had vigorously clubbed the Calvinistic doctrine of predestination, opening a debate that continues today. Who showed the more Christian grace in the dialogue, Whitefield or Wesley? The historians are divided on the matter. Perhaps both men could have taken a lesson from the Apostle Paul.

Yet another weakness of Whitefield was an early tendency to emphasize the size of the crowds at his meetings. Such entries in his journal may be explained by his youthfulness; after all, when God was using him to shake Philadelphia and Boston he was still only twenty-five years of age. As he grew older, Whitefield became more modest, reticent, and humble; but the statements in his early writings remain to create the image of an ego trip.

In 1739 Whitefield went to Bristol and asked permission to preach in the churches. He was refused. At that point he made a historic break by going out to nearby Kingswood on Saturday afternoon and preaching in the open air to the colliers fresh from the coal pits. The effect was incredible. G.H. Wicks has declared, "At Kingswood Whitefield broke the deadly decorum and spiritual lassitude of his age; there he began a new era in the religious life of England." Spurgeon told his students, "It was a brave day for England when Whitefield began field preaching." The dam was now broken; soon John and Charles Wesley were preaching in the open air, and the evangelical revival had begun.

In the year 1741 Whitefield married Elizabeth James, a widow ten years his senior. She bore him one child who died. Whitefield's marriage, while not as unfortunate as John Wesley's, was one which leaves questions unanswered. Extant letters indicate that George considered his evangelistic career above the building of a home.

Having said these things, one must come back with enthusiasm and admiration to the man and his work, the preacher and his message. What a selfless messenger of Christ he was! How I should like to have been in the crowd as George

Whitefield preached from the balcony of the Philadelphia Courthouse, to the thousands gathered on Market and Second streets.

"Father Abraham, " he cried, "whom have you in Heaven? Any Episcopalians?"

"No."

"Any Presbyterians?"

"No."

"Have you any Independents or Seceders?"

"No."

"Have you any Methodists?"

"No, no, no!"

"Whom have you there?"

"We don't know those names here! All who are here are Christians—believers in Christ—men who have overcome by the blood of the Lamb and the Word of His Testimony."

"Oh, is this the case? Then God help me, God help us all, to forget party names, and to become Christians in deed and in truth."

The Child-Catcher:

Amy Carmichael

Chapter Ten

It is a hot June day in South India early in the present century. Amy Carmichael, daughter of Ireland, has just published a best-seller about the temple traffic in children that has shocked the missionary world. Now she is seated at her type-writer in the mission compound at Dohnavur, four miles from a road, twenty-four miles from civilization.

A cough is heard outside the open door. "Come in."

Another cough. Amy rises and sees a shuffling form disappear around the corner of the house. She knows the man. She calls; he stops. What does he want? It seems he has reason to believe a female child is on its way to be dedicated to the god of a temple a day's journey away.

Amy knows what that means: a lifetime of servitude and religious prostitution. Already several children are living at Dohnavur who have been rescued from such a fate. "It would be well if she came here instead."

"If that is the Ammal's desire it may be possible to bring her."

"Could you overtake her?"

"She is waiting outside your gate."

A full hour later two temple women and a man finally approach the bungalow. They bring with them a fragile, sad-faced girl less than two years old. Knowing the ways of the East, Amy ignores the child and proceeds with the delicate negotiations. More hours pass. Tension rises. Suddenly one of the women snatches up the child and walks out the door.

Seeing a life hanging in the balance, Amy takes the initiative. She walks to the door and warns that God will repay, that someday he will punish sin. Startled, the woman rushes away, then returns and drops the child in Amy's arms. A paper is signed committing its permanent care to the Dohnavur Fellowship.

The scene shifts: it is now 1950. For nearly twenty years Amy Carmichael has been bedridden, as the result of a fall in the dark. She has written thirty-five books, thirteen of them while lying in pain. But the books have not all been about Dohnavur, or missions, or India. They have been about the Lord Jesus, his love and his faithfulness.

Expert medical help is attending her, but she is dying. She is eighty-two years old. The Dohnavur family she founded has grown to nearly a thousand. One hundred twenty older boys and girls are in training as teachers or nurses or are studying in Christian schools. Some are engaged in Christian work in other parts of India. Between forty and fifty missionary workers have come from the United Kingdom, Switzerland, Canada, and New Zealand to help. A hospital, called the "Place of Heavenly Healing," stands on the grounds, filled with patients. New converts and inquirers come daily for instruction in the Christian gospel.

All this has grown from the faith and devotion of a woman who in more than fifty-five years never took a furlough and never asked for money. Her biographer says she "was reverenced by the whole countryside." One of the hospital doctors, Nancy Robbins, gave her four words from the Revised Version of Revelation 2:9-10, "I know. . .fear not." Amy had them printed on wood and hung in her room under a light, so she could read them at night. Then she wrote, or rather dictated, these lines:

> *I know.* The words contain
> Unfathomable comfort for our pain.
> How they can hold such depths I do not know—
> I only know that it is so.
> *Fear not.* The words have power
> To give the Thing they name, for in an hour
> Of utter weariness the soul, aware

Of One beside her bed
Is comforted.
O Lord most dear,
I thank Thee, and I worship—Thou art here.

It was her last poem, completing a collection that has touched the hearts of unnumbered Christian believers around the world. Early on January 18, 1951, as her biographer, Frank Houghton, expressed it, she "passed through the Gates into the City." As soon as it became known, the bells in the forty-foot tower of the Dohnavur chapel, named the "House of Prayer," began to play the music of one of her songs. Fifteen hundred people filed by to pay their respects. She was buried in the churchyard, called "God's Garden," with no headstone. A beautiful stone birdbath was erected beside her grave.

Five years later a twenty-nine-year-old American missionary, Jim Elliot, was slain by an Auca Indian spear on a sandy beach of the Curaray river in Ecuador. (Four of his colleagues also died in the massacre.) In going through her late husband's diary Elliot's wife, Elisabeth, found poem after poem Jim had copied from the writings of Amy Carmichael.

But to think of her as simply an invalid poet, writing devotional thoughts, is to miss the major significance of Amy's life. For half a century she was God's chosen instrument, amazingly fitted for his purpose at a particular place and a particular time. She did something for the children of India that no one else was doing, or dreamt it possible to do.

The name "Amy Beatrice Carmichael" appears in the baptismal register of the Presbyterian Church at Ballycopeland, County Down, Northern Ireland, under the date January 19, 1868. Her ancestors had come from Ayrshire in Scotland. She was the eldest of seven children, and her first prayer was that her brown eyes might be changed to blue. But God knew what he was doing. In the years to come those brown eyes would let her into the Indian temple grounds in search of children, where blue eyes would have given her away. Long before other missionaries adopted the practice, Amy was wearing Indian dress; and on these surreptitious visits she stained her hands and arms with coffee.

As a young girl Amy attended a Wesleyan Methodist boarding school in Yorkshire for three years, then returned to Ireland and enrolled at a school in Belfast. By now the "wild Irish girl's" thoughts had begun to turn to God. She started teaching a Sunday morning class for "shawlies," Belfast mill-girls who wore shawls instead of hats. The work grew, and a larger hall was needed. Amy went to see the head of the largest mill in that part of Belfast, and he gave her a building practically rent-free. She named the place "The

Welcome," and opened it with a mission led by "two of Moody's students who happened to be in Belfast then." Soon a roaring program was in operation—Bible classes, singing practice, mothers' meetings, sewing club, night school, and gospel preaching—usually by Amy.

The loss of the family fortune scattered the family, and Amy went to Broughton Grange, England, to look after an elderly Christian, a friend of Hudson Taylor. There on the snowy night of January 13, 1892, at the age of twenty-four, she received God's call to the mission field in two words: "Go ye." She had no idea where she was to go, but a year later she sailed for Shanghai, hoping to join a Church Missionary Society work in Japan. Before the voyage was over she had led the captain of the S.S. *Valetta* to Christ.

Amy spent one year in Japan, during which she labored in Matsuye and Hirose, winning people to Christ despite the language barrier. To read her account *(From Sunrise Land)* is to sense the astonishing evangelistic gift God had bestowed upon her. She asked him for converts, and God provided them. It was in Japan she wrote the famous lines:

> O for a passionate passion for souls,
> O for a pity that yearns!
> O for the love that loves unto death,
> O for the fire that burns!
> O for the pure prayer-power that prevails,

That pours itself out for the lost!
Victorious prayer in the Conqueror's Name,
O for a Pentecost!

Called back to England by illness, Amy spent
nine months at Broughton Grange, and in the
spring of 1895 a letter came from a friend in Ban-
galore, South India, inviting her to work with the
Church of England Zenana Missionary Society
there. She was accepted on the basis of Keswick
support, and on November 9 she arrived in Ma-
dras. She never returned. As Bishop Houghton
said, "She loved India as few have loved it."

How does one compress into a few paragraphs
one of the most remarkable missionary stories of
all time? Amy quickly learned the Tamil language, studying it six hours a day. Her health was
never strong, and it was prophesied that she
would not last more than six months in India. She
received permission to move to Tinnevelly district
to improve her facility with Tamil. There she
formed a women's band which toured the villages
giving out the gospel. They were called the
"Starry Cluster" and traveled by bullock bandy,
visiting village homes and talking wherever there
were women or children ready to listen.

Then it happened. A Hindu girl in a mission
school was given a Bible and became a secret believer. She came to the mission bungalow at Pan-
naivilai early one morning, stood outside the ver-

anda and cried, "Refuge! Refuge!" Amy and her missionary teachers, the Walkers, took her in. The struggle was joined; relatives stormed the bungalow, for the girl was breaking caste. But she stood firm. The mission school and the teacher's house were burned, and the village turned its back on the Christian workers. But six months later another girl of the same caste escaped and came to the veranda crying, "Refuge!"

Amy breached missionary custom and kept the children with her. They moved to another village. An eleven-year-old girl heard the preaching and was drawn to Amy in her Indian dress. This was Arulai, who stayed with Amy and helped with the work for forty years until her death. Hindus began calling Amy "the child-catching Missie Ammal," and thought she drugged the children with a powder. One child who had responded was poisoned. Another was beaten and tied in a loft.

Then on March 6, 1901, a temple child escaped and was found by a Christian woman outside the church. She was brought to Amy. When the temple women appeared to claim her, the girl announced, "I won't go with them." The women could produce no evidence that the child was theirs, and the crisis passed. The child, Preena, told some stories of her life at the temple. Amy began to gather facts about the traffic in children for "temple service," and a new life began for her. She discovered an invisible network, by which children were "married to the gods" and left at the mercy of the priests. Boys and girls alike were involved, and the British government found itself unable to touch the sinister traffic.

Amy gathered her own corps of informants, and whenever it was rumored that a child was to be given to temple service (considered an act of religious merit) she arranged to have it brought to the new location at Dohnavur. The "Starry Cluster" expanded and settled down to become the Dohnavur Fellowship. Amy described her new work in one word—battle. Year after year the struggle went on, the babies came, and the work grew. It was one woman and her helpers against a gigantic evil system. But the word went out, and funds came in, and God gave his blessing.

Today the Dohnavur Fellowship continues its ministry for Christ, independent of all mission society affiliations, yet one in Christ with his servants everywhere. Amy Carmichael's body rests in India, but her books continue to sell, and she herself is with the Lord she loved so dearly. The curse of the children's traffic has been lifted by the Indian government; the pioneering protests of Amy Carmichael and other reformers finally bore fruit. What the British could not do, India herself has done. Meanwhile the ministry of love begun by Amy in the name of Christ for the land so beloved of her, goes on today in the power of Spirit and to the greater glory of God.